LYN ST. JAMES

LYN ST. JAMES

Driven to Be First

Ross R. Olney

 Lerner Publications Company • Minneapolis

To my friends, the Wishons, and especially Gig,
who reminds me of Lyn St. James in many ways.

Information for this book was obtained from the following sources:
500 Miles to Go by Al Bloemker; *Anderson (Indiana) Herald Bulletin;*
Avenues Magazine; Drama on the Speedway by Ross R. Olney; *Great
Moments in Speed* by Ross R. Olney; *How to Understand Auto Racing* by Ross
R. Olney; *Illustrated Auto Racing Dictionary for Young People* by Ross R.
Olney; *Indianapolis Motor Speedway; Indianapolis Star; Indianapolis Woman;
IndyCar Magazine; Lear's; Living Fit Magazine; Los Angeles Times; Lyn St.
James Motorsports; Open Wheel Magazine*, Editor Dick Berggren; *Sports Illus-
trated; Sunshine Magazine; Ventura County Star*

This book is available in two editions:
Library binding by Lerner Publications Company
Soft cover by First Avenue Editions
241 First Avenue North, Minneapolis, Minnesota 55401
International Standard Book Number: 0-8225-2890-8 (lib. bdg.)
International Standard Book Number: 0-8225-9749-7 (pbk.)

LIBRARY OF CONGRESS CATALOGING-IN-PUBLICATION DATA

Olney, Ross Robert, 1929–
Lyn St. James : driven to be first / Ross R. Olney
p.   cm. — (The achievers)
Summary: A biography of the race car driver who, in 1992, became the second
woman ever to participate in the Indianapolis 500 and the first ever to be named
rookie of the year in that race.
ISBN 0-8225-2890-8 (alk. paper). — ISBN 0-8225-9749-7 (alk. paper)
1. St. James, Lyn—Juvenile literature. 2. Women automobile racing drivers—
United States—Biography—Juvenile literature. [1. St. James, Lyn. 2. Automobile
racing drivers. 3. Women—Biography.]
I. Title. II. Series.
GV1032.S73056   1997
796.7'2'092—dc20
[B]   96–16239

Manufactured in the United States of America
1 2 3 4 5 6 – JR – 02 01 00 99 98 97

Contents

Lady *and* Gentlemen

Lyn St. James arrived early on race morning for her first Indianapolis 500. Calmly, she put on her fire-resistant racing suit. With a half hour to wait before the start of the race, she sat in her sleek race car, radio receiver earplugs and helmet in place. Like every other Indy driver, once she was in the car, the crowds faded from her mind. Although surrounded by pit crew members, photographers, 400,000 onlookers, and millions more on television, she retreated into thoughts of the next 500 miles.

Soon she would be blazing down the straightaway at more than 245 miles per hour, slicing down into 90-degree turns at nearly the same speed. She would be surrounded by 32 other drivers, the best in the world.

For years, she had driven in amateur races. She had driven go-karts and off-road racing cars. She had traveled untold thousands of miles, and made hundreds of telephone calls to potential sponsors. She had suffered discouragement and scorn from her male peers. She had proved herself again and again with race driving championships, and yet been turned away. After more than 10 years of dedication and determination, she had finally taken her place on the grid of the most famous motor race in the world.

The Indianapolis 500, or Indy 500, has 33 contestants each year. The drivers race in 11 rows of 3 drivers each. Practice for the Indy 500 starts at the beginning of May. The next two weekends are used for four-lap qualification runs. The pole position car is the fastest among the cars making the run on the first day. On the second of the four qualification days, other cars race. They fill in as a group behind the first-day qualifiers. Remaining cars run on the third day and finally the fourth day.

Often, the fourth day of qualifying becomes "bubble" day. Any car that is faster than a car already in the field is added to the race at the rear. The slower car is bumped out. Then everybody moves up one spot. By race morning, the faster cars are in place throughout the 33 cars.

Lyn St. James, once a very shy little girl who spent most of her time playing piano, was preparing to race at top speed at the Indianapolis Speedway on this May morning in 1992. She would be wheel to wheel at Indy with former winner Al Unser Senior and his son, Al Junior ("Little Al"). She would be racing the best drivers in the world. Just ahead of her in the starting field was A.J. Foyt. He is the race driver many fans call the greatest in the history of the sport.

Only two other women had ever attempted to race at Indy. Thirteen years before, Janet Guthrie had become the first woman ever at Indy when she made the field in 1977, '78 and '79. Desiré Wilson tried but was unable to qualify in 1982, '83 and '84. Whenever Guthrie appeared on the track or in the pits, a few people in the grandstands booed. Those people still believed that women didn't belong in Indy cars.

In 1976, Janet Guthrie drove in the Indianapolis 500. Shown with her are car owner Rolla Vollstedt, center, and her teammate, Dick Simon.

Desiré Wilson tried to qualify at Indy in 1982.

Less than 10 years before Guthrie drove, women weren't even allowed in the Indy garages. They weren't permitted in the pit section either. The Indy 500 was a men's race. No women were allowed.

Some fans in the 1940s believed in the "no women" rule so much that they were outraged when they saw the movie, *To Please a Lady*. The movie was about an Indy 500 driver, played by Clark Gable. In one scene, it appeared that Barbara Stanwyck's character was in the Indy garage area with Gable.

Racing fans protested until Indy officials admitted that Stanwyck had never actually entered the garage. A hole had been cut in the fence. Stanwyck had leaned through the hole, which made her appear to be in the garage. Indy officials insisted that her feet had stayed safely outside the all-male area.

As late as 1953, Bessie Lee Paoli, the owner of the second-place car, had to watch the race from the grandstands. Even a female car owner was not permitted in the pits or garages. By 1992, Lyn St. James knew that she *did* belong in these very powerful, very fast cars. Most racing fans agreed with her and cheered for her.

On that gray Sunday morning, May 24, 1992—the day before Memorial Day as always—the traditional starting command at the famous Indianapolis 500 was changed. Instead of *"Gentlemen,* start your engines," it was *"Lady* and gentlemen, start your engines."

The 1992 race was especially exciting. "Little Al" Unser beat Scott Goodyear to the line by only 0.43 of a second in the closest finish of this famous auto race's history. And, for the first time in Indianapolis 500 history, a father followed his winning son across the finish line. "Big Al" Unser placed third in the 1992 race.

Crashes eliminated 13 of the 33 drivers, starting on the parade lap. The parade lap is the lap before the start when the cars are going slowly as they line up in position. Roberto Guerrero, the fastest driver in the field, had impatiently stepped too hard on the gas pedal. His car's powerful engine spun the back wheels, and into the wall he went.

Lyn, a rookie, didn't crash. She placed 11th, beating out such top drivers as former 500 winners Rick Mears, Gordon Johncock, Emerson Fittipaldi, Arie Luyendyk, and Mario Andretti. For the first time in Indy history, a woman was chosen Rookie of the Year as the best new driver in the race.

Lyn was asked if it was difficult being a woman and a race driver. "I don't know what it would be like *not* to be a woman," she answered. "I don't have anything to compare it to. I'm proud to be a woman. I'm proud to be a driver.

"The car doesn't know the difference and no one can even see that it's a woman driving. No one judges me by my smile or personality, but by my results.

After the 1992 Indianapolis 500, Lyn St. James was named the Rookie of the Year at the awards banquet.

"There's no greater satisfaction in the world than driving down into Turn 1 when the car is right, with my foot flat on the pedal, knowing that I'm in the groove and feeling the bite as the tires grab hold going through the corner, then knowing I have the exact right amount of power coming out heading for the short chute," Lyn said. "Then, heading down into Turn 2, setting up for the long run down the back-straight. Oh, what a feeling!"

Eleven-year-old Evelyn enjoyed playing in her Willoughby, Ohio, neighborhood.

2

Concert Pianist or Grease Monkey?

Evelyn Cornwall was born in 1947. She was the only child of a Willoughby, Ohio, sheet metal worker, Alfred, and his wife, Maxine. A shy little girl, Evelyn attended a private school called the Andrews School for Girls. Evelyn's mother insisted that her daughter grow up a "lady." Little Evelyn was supposed to get married, raise children, and keep a house. But she happily learned mechanics from her father by helping him in his shop.

Evelyn never imagined that she would return to the school as a celebrity to deliver the 1992 commencement address. Nor did she consider herself an athlete during her school years. She fainted the first time she tried basketball. "I put my body in shock," she remembered, laughing. But she did play basketball, volleyball, and tennis in school.

"I wrote myself off because I was too shy," she told *Indianapolis Woman Magazine*. "Andrews taught me how to live with other kids. In public high school, all I could have been was a cheerleader, and I wouldn't have made the cheerleading squad. Sports taught me that just because things aren't going right doesn't mean people are picking on you. I never could have related with my all-male racing teams if I hadn't learned that."

As a young girl, Evelyn spent most of her spare time practicing piano. She took lessons for 13 years and was good enough to attend the St. Louis Institute of Music. She thought of becoming a concert pianist.

As a youngster, Evelyn dreamed of being a concert pianist.

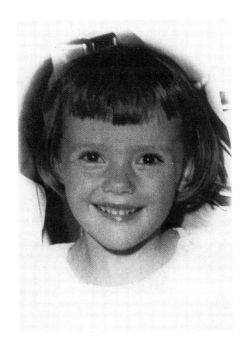

Evelyn was shy as a child and liked quiet activities best.

"I was self-conscious all through grade school," she admitted. "I didn't have many friends. I never felt good about my looks. I wasn't one of those girls who wants to spend an hour and a half getting dressed in the morning to look my best. If there was any person I wanted to be like, it was my piano teacher. She was a beautiful human being. She dressed perfectly and she was always sweet."

According to her mother, "The piano didn't seem to give her enough." Even though Evelyn dreamed of being a concert pianist, "She had it in her head, but [not] in her hands," said her mother.

Evelyn and her mother, Maxine, pose for a photograph.
Maxine taught Evelyn how to drive.

Still, the mother encouraged the daughter's interest
in music as the father encouraged her in machines.
Evelyn's mother also influenced her in another way
that dramatically changed Evelyn's life. Maxine

Cornwall had been sick with polio when she was a child. She had trouble walking as a result of the disease. Maxine drove a car everywhere, and taught her 16-year-old daughter how to drive.

Maxine also took Evelyn to watch the Indy 500 race in 1966. The two sat in the vast grandstands outside Turn 1. Just after the start, there was a terrible accident. Billy Foster's car slammed into the outside wall. This set off a chain-reaction crash, and 11 cars were out of the race. Some of them screeched to a smoking stop directly in front of Evelyn and her shocked mother. Dazed, A.J. Foyt jumped from his smashed car and crawled over the high-wheel fence, right in front of Evelyn and her mom.

"There were parts flying all over the place and total devastation. It was frightening," recalled Evelyn. For most people, that probably would have been the end of dreaming about driving in the 500. "But when I left," she insisted, "I remembered the excitement and the sounds of the engines.

"I had a dream, a fantasy at that point," she said. "I pursued it. I wasn't that cocky to say that I'm going to be out there with those guys someday. But I said it sort of inside, as a dream."

At private school, Evelyn Cornwall's friends were girls. Outside school, her friends were mostly boys. Boys are often interested in cars. Evelyn loved the piano, but she discovered that she also loved cars and engines. She didn't mind getting grease under her fingernails, and she loved driving fast.

As a teenager, she enjoyed working on engines, but, "The first time I tore an engine down and put it back together, I had a whole box of parts left over. I was discouraged," she admitted, "until a mechanic told me, 'Aw, it happens all the time.' I felt better."

When she was 17, she teased one of her friends because he lost a drag race. The friend challenged her to "put up or shut up." So, the group of teenagers hurried off to the drag strip, and Evelyn jumped into the car. She won her very first race. "I won a trophy," she recalled with pride.

Her mother was not happy. "You're not going to do that again," she ordered. For the next 10 years, young Evelyn didn't.

The Cornwall family was not wealthy, so Evelyn passed on college and took a job as a secretary at U.S. Steel in Cleveland. She also earned money by teaching piano lessons to children.

Evelyn Cornwall's first name change came when she married John Carusso in 1970. She met Carusso while at U.S. Steel, and they soon realized that they both loved cars and racing. John owned an electronics business in Hallandale, Florida, so they moved there and became partners in the company.

Evelyn Carusso was an excellent businesswoman, and the company prospered. In 1973, after John took a racing driver's education course, he and Evelyn bought a Ford Pinto to compete in regional amateur Sports Car Club of America (SCCA) races.

Evelyn became a helper on her husband's racing team. When John moved to a Corvette in SCCA racing, Evelyn took over the Pinto. The SCCA was one of the first organizations to allow women to compete. Evelyn attended two SCCA driving schools, earned her competition license, and was eager and ready for her first race.

The race was not a success. Evelyn lost control of the Pinto in a corner. The car spun wildly off the track and sank in a trackside lake. Evelyn nearly drowned before track workers got to the scene and rescued her. "It was very embarrassing and very frustrating," she recalled.

But she didn't quit. She continued to drive the Pinto in SCCA races. Then she bought a faster Chevrolet Vega, and in 1976 and '77 she was the SCCA Florida Regional Champion in the showroom stock class. By 1978, she had become runner-up in Southeast SCCA competition. She also drove her husband's Corvette in the famous 12-hour race at Sebring, Florida. Evelyn Carusso was becoming a good race car driver.

But she wasn't happy being just "Mrs. Carusso," wife of the "real" driver on the team. In spite of her victories on the racetrack, she was still the one the mechanics called on to go for parts or prepare sand-wiches. "I was a great 'gofer,' " she recalled. "When-ever they needed bolts or some part fabricated, or a piece of pipe or tubing, I was the one who was sent out to find it. You know, send out a young woman and you get the part."

Staying in shape became more important to Evelyn as she became more involved with sports car racing.

Most amateur racers work at full-time jobs, then spend every off-duty moment on their cars. They put every penny they can into their racing operation. When they can afford to, or if they want to move up a class, they buy a more expensive car and then put more money into it. Some racers drive closed cars, such as those seen on the street. Others choose open-cockpit cars. That's what Evelyn dreamed of driving.

The Carusso marriage continued to be strained since both partners wanted to drive. In 1979, the Carussos divorced. Evelyn was on her own. She had to finance her cars herself, look for sponsors herself, and serve as her own team manager. At Andrews School, the teachers had taught the girls to be self-reliant, to go for a goal, to aim high. So Evelyn opened an auto parts store. It was a successful and profitable store and she continued to own and manage it until 1992 when she sold it.

Evelyn Carusso also decided that, at age 32, she needed another name change. She enjoyed the television show *McMillan and Wife*, so she telephoned actress Susan St. James. Evelyn had always loved the last name, St. James. She asked Susan for permission to use that name. Susan St. James gave her permission, so Evelyn legally changed her name to Lyn St. James.

Getting in the Race

After her divorce in 1979, Lyn often had to work very hard as she forged ahead alone on her racing career. She had many exciting and happy times, but she also faced sad moments. Still, she found strength within herself to keep working toward her goal.

One event in 1980 was very difficult for Lyn, but it also made her stronger. Lyn had brought her beloved Irish setter, Max, to a race at the Palm Beach International Raceway in Florida. Although he hated being on a leash, Max was kept tied up so that he would be safe among all the race cars moving around the pit area. Finally, the day's events ended and Lyn allowed her pet off his leash for a run along the track.

"He looked so beautiful with his furry red coat fluttering like feathers as he ran onto the track," Lyn recalled sadly. "Suddenly I saw a car speeding down the track. I waved my arms and yelled to the driver that a dog was on the track, but it was too late."

Lyn heard a thud as the car hit her dog. She rushed Max to a veterinarian, but early the next morning, the beautiful dog died.

"I have never cried so much in my life," said Lyn. "I just wanted to go home. Later that day, though, I decided I would try to race. That was my job. During the pace lap, I drove right over the spot where Max had been hit and I got choked up. I started to close my eyes, but then my competitive instincts clicked on. I focused on the race."

Lyn remembers that the moment she took her helmet off, she started crying again. But she also remembers that losing her dog taught her that she could get through a tough time. She learned to concentrate on her work or other responsibilities when she was sad.

Lyn had plenty of responsibilities. By 1981, she was driving a Mercury Capri. She had to pay for her car herself and look for sponsors for each race. She had to manage the racing team and arrange for pit workers. She had to do everything—and then drive, too. Meanwhile, the men she was racing against merely arrived at the track and raced. They had sponsorship money and helpers to do all the other chores.

In 1981, Lyn finished in fifth place in the championship point standings for her car class. But nothing seemed to go right in 1982. Even the most optimistic person, in any career, can begin to feel discouraged.

Lyn drove a specially made Mercury Capri during the 1981 racing season.

Lyn and her Capri were successful in 1981, but the 1982 season was not a good one for Lyn.

Lyn wondered if a woman really did belong in bigtime racing. Maybe, she began to think, the odds of a woman making it in racing really were too great to overcome.

"I began to consider myself a total failure," she recalled. "You know, men can just be sitting around having a beer together, and one of them is a race car driver and the other is a race car owner, and the next thing you know the owner says to the driver, 'Hey, I want you to drive my car.' That chemistry, that almost indescribable thing that men have, is pretty tough for a woman driver to re-create."

Then she saw a magazine article about famed National Association for Stock Car Auto Racing (NASCAR) driver Bobby Allison. "The article was about Bobby winning the NASCAR driving championship," Lyn said. "In it, he said that in 22 years of racing he had gone through 17 different racing teams. It made me realize that maybe this was the way the game was played, and that I wasn't the one at fault."

In 1984, *Autoweek* magazine named Lyn Rookie of the Year in International Motor Sports Association (IMSA) Grand Touring (GT) racing. This award, and many letters and telephone calls to Ford Motor Company executives, persuaded Ford to sponsor Lyn in 10 IMSA GT races.

Lyn's career took off. She won 3 of the 10 races and placed well in others. One of the high points of her racing career was in a 1985 IMSA GT race at Watkins Glen, New York. But even that race caused controversy.

Drivers share the job in GT cars. Lyn's codriver was Whitney Ganz, a man who was just as eager to drive as Lyn was. She roared into the pits for the team's final pit stop in the 500-kilometer race. A driver change was scheduled, but she didn't move. Ganz tried to help unhook her seat belts, but she stared straight ahead. She didn't want to get out of the car. With pit service finished, she thundered back into the race.

"I wasn't tired, and I didn't need relief," she said bluntly. She took the checkered flag, and the reporters surrounded her. Normally this is also a great moment for the crew of the winning car. Crew members usually swarm around and get their pictures taken, as they deserve. Not a single member of Lyn's crew appeared at the victory celebration. They were upset that she had "hogged" the glory. Later, Whitney Ganz took her aside and said that he wouldn't have given up the car either.

Race driver Emory Donaldson, a longtime friend of Lyn's, said, "Lyn never asked for respect; she went out and earned it on the track. You put her in a first-rate car, and she's going to win."

Lyn drove a number 07 Ford Probe research vehicle to a women's closed-course speed record at Alabama International Speedway in 1985. The record still stands at 204.223 miles per hour (mph).

"At that speed," said Lyn, "you are driving the car at its absolute limits. Your visual reference points come up so much quicker. I felt like I was threading a needle. I wasn't frightened, but I can tell you it was eerie. At those speed levels, the car just takes over. That's where my own aggressiveness comes in."

Lyn set 31 national and international speed records for women, including a lap of 212.577 mph at Talladega Speedway in Bill Elliott's NASCAR racer. She was clocked at 232 mph through a straightaway speed trap. She was 38 years old that year, 1985. "But remember, that was in a coupe with sheet metal all around me," Lyn said. "All of my 16 years of racing have been in cars with a roof over my head. [Car owner] Dick [Simon] knew I needed to get the feel of the air rushing past me, so he took me to Texas World Speedway where I lapped at over 220 [miles per hour]."

Lyn wears an unusual "07" necklace in honor of the Probe, but she took something else away from the experience as well. Lyn learned that she needed muscles to race. The Probe had been perfectly set up for a record attempt and didn't demand much in the way of strength from the driver. When she raced the car the next season, Lyn said it felt like "an elephant had put his foot" on it on the curves and straightaways and in the close racing on a track. Since then, she has had a personal trainer to keep her in physical shape to handle high-speed cars.

Most race car drivers work hard at being fit. They point out that driving a high-speed car on the ragged edge for hours at a time demands the strength, endurance and total concentration of a perfectly conditioned athlete.

The forces of gravity brought on by accelerating from 50 to 150 mph in a stretch of 500 yards puts an intense backward strain on a driver's head and neck. So do the side forces that build up and push the driver one way or the other on long-radius turns at speeds of 200 mph.

If a driver is using a manual transmission and shifting hundreds or even thousands of times during a race, there is added strain. All of this is happening as the cockpit temperature rises to 140 degrees. Then there is the emotional pressure of trying to go faster than many other fast cars. Race car drivers must be well conditioned, especially if they are really planning to win.

Top race car drivers, like Lyn, have to work out to stay fit.

As Lyn won more races and set more records, she began to get better, more advanced, cars to drive. The car in the photo above is one that Lyn drove while setting a record.

Lyn is 5 feet 6 inches tall and weighs 125 pounds. She credits Human Performance International, a mind and body testing organization in Daytona Beach, Florida, with keeping her mentally and physically fit.

Lyn uses visualization, or imagery, to prepare mentally for a race. She sees herself driving the car the way she wants to be driving it, doing what she must do to win. She has an electrically powered race car tub, or body, in her apartment. She sits in the "cockpit" for hours, moving the steering wheel and pushing the pedals, visualizing a victory. The device is similar to virtual reality games in arcades. But instead of seeing things on a screen, you move the pressurized wheel and pedals and see them in your head. The device is hooked up to computer monitors so specific conditions at specific tracks can be duplicated. Lyn can "drive" race after race under realistic conditions. There is even a blower so she can feel warm air rushing past the cockpit. "I don't care what people think," she said. "I'm trying to do everything in my power to be prepared . . . for the most important race in the world."

Being mentally and physically fit doesn't guarantee that a driver will not crash. Accidents do happen on the racetrack. One happened to Lyn in a 1986 GT race at the Riverside International Raceway in California. Her speeding car hit the Riverside wall at more than 180 mph after being bumped. Immediately, Lyn's out-of-control car was struck by several other racers as it careened back across the track.

Then Lyn's racer flipped upside down and bounced wildly, metal screaming against the track surface. When the racer finally stopped in a great cloud of dust and falling car parts, it burst into flames. There seemed to be no way a driver could survive such a dreadful crash. The crowd watching the race was stunned into silence.

Many organizations, such as this girl's Girl Scout troop, have honored Lyn for her achievements.

Fire trucks and ambulances rushed to the scene to attend to several smashed cars and Lyn's burning car. Suddenly she could be seen crawling through the wall of flames engulfing the racer. Fans began to cheer as she stood and walked slowly away, heading toward a nearby telephone to call her mother. The race was being shown on national television, and she didn't want her mother to worry. Although Lyn suffered two herniated disks in her back in the terrible Riverside crash, she was soon racing again.

Lyn continued to struggle in auto racing. Some male drivers still made fun of her, although she drove on the winning teams in the 1987 24 Hours of Le Mans and the 1990 24 Hours of Daytona. These are major long-distance motor racing events where a team of drivers shares the work over the 24-hour period. Most of the time, however, Lyn was still doing *everything* on her own racing team, including driving.

Lyn and her team won the challenging 24 Hours of Daytona race in 1990.

Finding Support

Going fast wasn't the problem for Lyn. Her most difficult challenge was to find a sponsor to pay for driving at Indianapolis. Each driver in the Indy 500 must arrange for hundreds of thousands of dollars of sponsorship. With the money in hand, the driver then contacts car owners. If the driver has won before, prominent car owners are approached. Car owners are more likely to choose a driver who has a winning record—or a lot of sponsorship money.

"No one said the world was fair," Lyn admitted. "It's funding that drives the wheels of the sport." After hiring a manager to run her store, Lyn spent most of her time on the road, seeking sponsorships. Although she had a great smile and a winning attitude, she was still hampered by her shyness. She was not comfortable meeting with strangers and asking for help, but she kept at it.

For two years, she contacted more than 150 companies, asking for sponsorship money. Ford, which had been her sponsor, already had big-name drivers like Michael Andretti. Some of Lyn's friends had collected $10,000, but that wasn't nearly enough to field an Indy race car. She needed 10 times that amount just to get started at Indy.

Then, six weeks before the 1992 Indy 500, Lyn finally won sponsorship from J. C. Penney Co. The Agency Rent-a-Car company also joined her team. Her sleek Indy car was painted with the slogan of a Penney's advertising campaign, "Spirit of the American Woman." Officials from Penney's later said that the $100,000 they invested in Lyn resulted in publicity that was worth about $2.7 million in advertising.

Lyn's pit crew gets her back on track during the 1992 Indianapolis 500.

Lyn concentrated on the job ahead. "This is a goal I've had in meeting a career objective," Lyn explained. "Everything I've done in the past 10 or 12 years professionally has been in preparation for this."

Still, her rookie tryout wasn't easy. Lyn had almost no experience in open-wheeled, open-cockpit cars. She had driven a few laps in 1988 at a Memphis speedway. Then, in 1990, she drove a car for 50 laps at Indy on a practice day. That was her entire open-cockpit experience.

Experienced Indy drivers watch and judge a rookie as he or she drives around the Indianapolis track at various specific speeds in a rookie trial. The veteran drivers then decide whether the rookie is ready to race. "I drove very cautiously," Lyn said. "I just got acquainted with the place."

Lyn drove too fast, though. She drove seven miles an hour over the rookie speed limit. Several times, officials waved a black flag to call her into the pits and insist that she be more careful. Said car owner Dick Simon, who was watching, "I gained a lot of respect for her, the way she held her temper. She showed a lot of professionalism." Simon had helped Janet Guthrie race at Indy, and Lyn later drove one of his cars, too.

Janet Guthrie, a racing pioneer, and Lyn compare stories.

Although Lyn was already aware of the great danger of her profession, a crash during a practice run that year emphasized how careful drivers must be. Another rookie, Jovy Marcelo, lost control while driving at a high speed and smashed into the wall. He was killed in the crash.

The first driver back on the track after the debris had been cleared was Lyn St. James. "[Racing] is a calculated risk," she admitted. "You don't just casually get in the car. It's not all guts and no brains.

"Unfortunately, I have seen other drivers killed," Lyn said. "The first time it ever happened to me was at West Palm Beach. I went up and talked to the driver's wife. I said, 'You don't know me and I don't know you, but I can tell you as a driver he was killed doing what he loves to do.' "

The day after Marcelo's accident, Lyn took to the track for a qualification run. She was driving a new 750-horsepower, Chevrolet-powered car. Each of her four laps was faster than the one before.

Lyn qualified for the race with a blazing speed of 220.150 mph in front of 100,000 roaring fans on the third of four qualifying days. Low car numbers are assigned according to where a driver finished in the previous year's races. Other drivers can ask for other numbers. Nobody had asked for number 90, so Lyn used it in honor of the J. C. Penny 90th birthday celebration.

"I love cars and I love racing," said Lyn. "It's an absolute honor to be in the field at the Indianapolis 500. This is absolutely the best day of my life."

Race driver Bobby Rahal was quoted in the *Los Angeles Times* about Lyn's 1992 qualification run. "She did a wonderful job," said the former Indy winner. According to Simon, "When the drivers line up alongside Lyn, they're not gun-shy at all. They have all the respect in the world for her." Johnny Capels, Executive Vice President of the United States Auto Club said, "Lyn understands what is expected of any Indy Car driver. She is . . . well received by the public."

Women were especially proud of her. A huge newspaper message appeared in the *Indianapolis Star* before the 1992 Indy race. Hollywood film director Penny Marshall and the "Girls of Summer" had paid for the ad. This group made the motion picture *A League of Their Own* with Madonna and Tom Hanks. The message read, "You are *definitely* in a league of your own!"

5

Full Speed Ahead

Lyn's first Indy 500 was marred by accidents. She skillfully maneuvered around them, time after time. She was the only rookie still running at the end.

"I thought the race would end it," her mother said after the race. "She said if she could get in, that was all she wanted. But now she's going for [next year]. She's a very determined girl."

After a full year of racing on the Indy-car circuit, Lyn qualified for the 1993 Indy 500. She drove from 21st place to 15th place before her car stalled with transmission problems on lap 177. She finally finished in 25th place, but she still won $161,212 for herself and her car owner.

Lyn affected the 1993 race even after her car failed. As wreckers rushed to remove her stalled car from the track, the field bunched up behind the pace car and leader Nigel Mansell. When the green flag flew with only a few laps left, shrewd Emerson Fittipaldi was prepared. He took advantage of newcomer Mansell's inexperience and rocketed past him. Directly on Fittipaldi's rear wing was former winner Arie Luyendyk. He also shot past the startled English champion. Fittipaldi won the race soon after, with Luyendyk second and Mansell third.

Lyn changed her name again in 1993, although racing fans will always know her as "St. James." She married Colorado land developer Roger Lessman and became the proud stepmother of Lessman's 10-year-old daughter, Lindsay. The two auto racing enthusiasts met at a race when Lessman, a driver of land-speed-record cars, chatted with Lyn about driving to a new land-speed record (LSR) in a car he helped design. LSR cars are superstreamlined and built to go as fast as possible in a straight line, often at the salt flats in Utah. Lyn says Lessman wasn't overwhelmed by her at their first meeting. "Heck, total strangers hug me. From Roger, I got a handshake," she said, laughing.

At the 1994 Indy, Lyn qualified with the sixth-fastest time. She was on the outside of the second row in a J. C. Penney/Reebok/Lee Jeans 1994 Lola/Ford Cosworth XB. No longer was she driving "old" race cars, as she had been doing before. No longer was she known as a "woman driver." She was a *race* driver. In 1994, she qualified faster than world champion Nigel Mansell and former Indy 500 winners Arie

Lyn and her stepdaughter, Lindsay, play on a snowmobile as Lyn's husband, Roger, watches. Lyn and Roger both like to race cars, snowmobiles, and other vehicles.

Luyendyk, Mario Andretti, and Bobby Rahal.

"I hope [the qualification run] continues to strengthen the importance women's sports have in society," Lyn said. "The fact is that I don't compete against just women. But that isn't the issue. The issue is to be a player, and not just a spectator."

During the race, Lyn's car ran over some debris from a wreck. This caused a long pit stop and handling problems throughout the rest of the race. She drove steadily and smoothly while she was on the track and finally managed to finish 19th.

Lyn points out that "racing luck" plays a big part in the sport. You might be winning the race, and run over a tiny piece of a car from a wreck. This could punch a hole in your radiator, or flatten a tire, and you must drop out. You might hit a car that is spinning in front of you, or become involved in an accident through no fault of your own. All drivers understand that the Indianapolis Speedway can be a very cruel racetrack, sometimes punishing a driver for no apparent reason

No longer shy, Lyn signs autographs for her racing fans.

at all, because of the very high speeds.

Later in 1994, during a qualifying run at the Michigan International Speedway, Lyn set a women's closed-course speed record of 224.208. She was going faster and faster, and becoming more and more well known in racing.

Even though she didn't have a sponsor in 1995, Lyn came to Indianapolis hoping to find one. J. C. Penney had dropped out of racing. Finally, Lyn arranged sponsorship from Whitlock Auto Parts and, on the third qualification day, she made the race in one of Dick Simon's cars. She qualified even though she had just two days of practice in the new car, a 1995 Lola/Ford. Lyn beat her own record with a second lap of 225.722 mph.

Lyn brushed against the wall during the third lap of her qualification run. Streaking along at top speed, she moved up a little too high in the "short chute" between the first and second turns. The tires of her car touched the wall. Rubber smoke puffed out. A black mark appeared on the white wall. Spectators braced themselves for what they were certain was coming. When a car touches the Indy wall it almost always spins out of control. The speeding car should have crashed. Lyn streaked on.

"She did such a nice job," Simon said with a broad smile. "To miscalculate by half an inch after not having any laps on the track is no sin. One of the things she proved to a lot of the men is that when anybody touches the wall at Indy, their next lap is way down, [but] hers was almost the same."

At 48, Lyn was the oldest active driver to qualify for the field. With a grin, she cheered for Emerson Fittipaldi to qualify. Fittipaldi is three months older than Lyn. "Emerson promised me that he would not quit racing until I quit, because I don't want to be known as the 'oldest driver' in the sport," Lyn an-

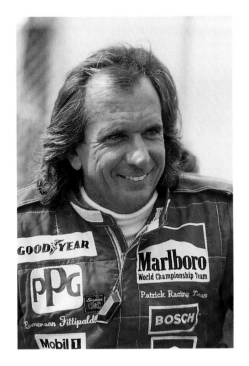

Emerson Fittipaldi, an Indy 500 winner, has raced against Lyn for many years.

nounced with a grin.

But, for the first time in history, the previous year's winner did not make the field. The Penske team cars were expected to dominate in 1995. They had won the previous two races on the Indy-car circuit. Their cars were being driven by former Indy winners Fittipaldi and Al Unser Jr. But the Penske team couldn't fix problems with the cars, and neither Fittipaldi nor Unser Jr. made the race.

Race day 1995 dawned cloudy after a night of rain. Lyn arrived early to prepare for what she thought was

her best chance ever to win an Indianapolis 500. She had qualified well, and she had a brand-new, perfectly running car. As always, even with clouds in the sky, hundreds of thousands of fans filled the vast Indianapolis Speedway grandstands and infield. Everybody knew the drivers would go fast at the beginning. It could start to rain again, and the one in the lead would be the winner if the race was more than half over when rain forced them to stop.

Racers must drive two or three seconds ahead of themselves at most tracks, but especially at Indy. They need that much time to react to a problem. Lyn knew something else that most racing fans don't consider. Starting back in the field, she would have to fight off the effects of fumes from burning methanol fuel for the first few laps, while the cars were bunched. Methanol fumes can make a driver dizzy.

With another "*Lady* and Gentlemen, Start Your Engines!" the 1995 race began. Thirty-three of the fastest, most colorful cars, driven by the best drivers in the world, roared under the green flag toward the first turn. Lyn pressed down on the gas pedal. She was going to try to win.

Seconds later, she was sitting in her wrecked car, out of the race. When reporters asked her what happened, she answered, "I'm not sure. I'd like to see a replay of it myself. It happened far ahead."

Up front in the field, as the cars roared into the

first turn of the first lap, Stan Fox's car suddenly veered to the right. Fox glanced off Eddie Cheever's car, then slammed hard into the wall. Cheever's car ripped Fox's car in two. The back half, with Fox still strapped in, bounced into the air, and slammed the wall again. Then Fox and Cheever slid side by side to a smoking stop. Behind, cars zigged this way and that, bumping into other sliding, bouncing cars. The crash was strikingly similar to the one in 1966, when Lyn and her mother had been spectators sitting on the other side of the very same wall. This time, Lyn was *in* the terrible crash.

"I thought I picked a hole to get through up high," said Lyn later, "but I got into the wall. Those things shouldn't happen, but they do."

Several other cars were out of the race because of the crash. Fox was taken by helicopter to Indianapolis Methodist Hospital where he underwent brain surgery. He was in the hospital for many weeks before he finally recovered from the crash.

Lyn, dejected and shaken but uninjured, watched the rest of the 1995 race from the pits. Canadian Jacques Villeneuve, a second-year driver at Indy and son of Grand Prix Champion Gilles Villeneuve, finally won the 1995 race.

Lyn continues to drive in other forms of motor racing also, including off-road races in the desert. Although Lyn is the fastest woman ever in racing, she isn't the fastest driver in her family. Her husband ran 292.719 in a land-speed-record car at Bonneville. Lyn plans to better the piston-driven-engine (not jet powered, but an engine like the one in the family car) land speed record. The piston record is the one many auto enthusiasts consider to be the real land speed record. The record of 409.9 mph is held by driver Al Teague, but Lyn and her husband are having a sleek car built. Their car, also designed by Indy car builder Bob Riley, will be driven at the Bonneville Salt Flats

A go-kart is another vehicle Lyn likes to drive—and race.

and will be fueled by natural gas.

Many women are proud of Lyn, and not just because of her racing. Lyn works with the Girls, Inc. Eureka Program, a summer science, math, and sports achievement program. One year, she helped girls build and race four Soap Box Derby cars. She received the Touchstone Award in 1992 for her work

Lyn encourages girls to participate in racing by helping the Girls, Inc., Soap Box Derby contestants.

with Girls, Inc.

Lyn was president of the Women's Sports Foundation from 1990 to 1993, and founded the Lyn St. James Foundation in 1993. The foundation is an educational organization that focuses on worldwide activities and programs for automotive safety and driver development, especially for aspiring women race car drivers.

Lyn also launched the Make a Difference campaign in 1994. She gives some of her racing prize money to programs in the Indianapolis area that offer opportunities for girls through sports and leadership development.

Nor has she lost her talent at the piano. Often she sits down at the family's baby grand piano and plays beautiful Chopin or Beethoven pieces.

"Actually, the discipline I've learned sitting at the piano all these years, repeating the same piece over and over until it's perfect, has helped me with driving," said Lyn. "I think of the metronome. Once you're out on the track and you've achieved your speed and established your reference points, you just get into the rhythm and go."

If she wins or, as Lyn says, *when* she wins the Indy 500, most of the stereotypes about auto racing will finally disappear. Sponsors will put more money and resources behind her and other women in professional sports. But, to her, the matter is more personal.

"I know where I come from in my heart as a racing driver," she said. "I want to win [the Indy 500], and

Lifetime Television became Lyn's sponsor in 1996. Below, with part of the hood removed, the high-tech engine in Lyn's car is visible.

I'm not going to worry about what happens if I do. People think big-time racing is, 'Ah man, let's go out there and kick butt,' but it isn't. It's the epitome of competitive, strategic war out there."

When Lyn thinks back to her first Indy 500, she smiles. She remembers one *Sports Illustrated* reader who followed her career. The magazine almost ignored her in their 1992 Indy 500 race coverage, when she was still an unknown in auto racing. Furious, the reader sent the editor a simple letter that said only, "Gentlemen, cancel my subscription." The editor needed no further explanation.

"It hasn't been an easy road to go down," she said. "I've had some real lows along the way. But two thoughts always come to mind. First, no one is holding a gun to my head to make me do this; it's my choice. Second, the sheer thrill and joy of driving the race car is what keeps me going. I have never quit believing in myself."

Glossary

black flag: Race officials wave flags to signal drivers. A black flag means the driver should go to the pit area.

checkered flag: Indicates the race is over. The driver who is first at that time wins.

chute: A straightaway, or straight part of the track. Also, a parachute used to slow a drag racer at the end of the strip.

closed course: A permanent track, not on city streets or off-road.

drag race: A high-speed race on a quarter-mile course between two cars racing side by side on a drag strip.

drag strip: A quarter-mile course wide enough for two cars to race side by side.

green flag: Tells racers that they can go fast because the track ahead is clear.

GT: Grand Touring, meaning that the car is specially built to race.

high-wheel fence: A mesh or wire fence above the walls to hold rolling wheels inside the track, away from spectators.

Indy car: An open-cockpit car built to race in the Indianapolis 500 and at other, similar races.

Indy-car circuit: The series of races that are contested by Indy car drivers.

infield: The area enclosed by a racetrack.

lap: One complete circuit of the racetrack.

land-speed record: A type of racing where drivers try to achieve the fastest possible speed while driving in a straight line.

manual transmission: The type of transmission that requires a driver to shift into different gears depending upon speed and track conditions.

open-cockpit car: A car in which the driver is not enclosed by body panels.

pace car: Often a standard passenger car that leads a field of racing cars into a flying start.

parade lap: A lap before the flying start, when fans can see the cars and cheer the drivers.

pit stop: A stop during a race when a racing team refuels the car, changes the tires, and does anything else that is needed to keep the car running.

pit: An area off the track where racers come in for service during the race. Also called the pit area or pit section.

qualifying: Runs to earn positions in the starting field. Generally, the faster a driver qualifies, the better his or her position for the start.

Career Highlights

Indy Car Statistics

Starts	8
Top-10 qualifying	2
Top-15 finishes	2

- Won 1992 Indy 500 Rookie of the Year (only woman ever to win)
- Set the national closed-course speed record for the fourth time, reaching 224.282 mph at the 1994 Indy 500 qualification
- Qualified sixth for the 1994 Indy 500 (highest ever for a woman)

SCCA Trans-Am Statistics

Starts	53
Top-5 finishes	7
Top-10 finishes	23

- Third place at Long Beach in 1988 (highest for a woman in series history)

IMSA GT Statistics

Starts	62
Wins	6
Top-5 finishes	17
Top-10 finishes	37

- Only woman ever to have won IMSA GT class
- First woman ever to have won IMSA driving solo.

Major Awards and Honors

- 1984 IMSA Rookie of the Year
- 1985 IMSA Norelco Driver of the Year
- 1986 *McCall's* Woman of the Year
- 1987 U.S. Girls Scouts Leadership Award
- 1988 SCCA Gordon Smiley Award
- 1992 Indy 500 Rookie of the Year
- 1992 ABC's Person of the Week
- 1994 Florida Sports Hall of Fame Inductee

ACKNOWLEDGMENTS

Photographs are reproduced with the permission of: p. 1, Mary Ann Carter/LSJ Motorsports; pp. 6, 11, 13, 14, 16, 17, 18, 22, 24, 27, 28, 30, 33, 34, 36, 37, 41, 42, 44, 49, 51, 54, 57, LSJ Motorsports; p. 2, Indianapolis Motor Speedway/Dave Edelstein; pp. 9, 10, UPI/Corbis-Bettmann; p. 38, Indianapolis Motor Speedway/Linda McQueeney; p. 40, Indianapolis Motor Speedway/Dave Wiloughby; p. 46, Les Welch/LSJ Motorsports; p. 50, Peter H. Bick/LSJ Motorsports; p. 53, SportsChrome East/West; p. 58, Sid Rust Photography/LSJ Motorsports; p. 60 (both), RRM Productions Inc./Robert Moody.

Front cover photograph of Lyn St. James by Indianapolis Motor Speedway/Ron McQueeney. Front cover photograph of Lyn St. James' car by AllSport/Steve Swope Racing Photos. Back cover photograph by Ted Wood/LSJ Motorsports. Artwork by John Erste.